Food and Festivals

A Flavour of

THE CARIBBEAN

Linda Illsley

WAYLAND

Other titles:

Cover photograph: Selling fruit on a market stall in Jamaica.

Title page: Traditional dancers in Jamaica.

Contents page: Drinking the sweet milk of a coconut.

All Wayland books encourage children to read and help them improve their literacy.

✓ The contents page, page numbers, headings and index help locate specific pieces of information.

✓ The glossary reinforces alphabetic knowledge and extends vocabulary.

✓ The further information section suggests other books dealing with the same subject.

✓ Find out more about how this book is specifically relevant to the National Literacy Strategy on page 31.

First published in 1998 by
Wayland Publishers Ltd, 61 Western Road, Hove,
East Sussex, BN3 1JD, England

© Copyright 1998 Wayland Publishers Ltd

Series editor: Polly Goodman
Book editor: Alex Edmonds
Designer: Mark Whitchurch
Picture researcher: Paula Chapman

British Library Cataloguing in Publication Data
Illsley, Linda
 A Flavour of the Caribbean. – (Food and festivals)
 1. Festivals – Caribbean Area – Juvenile literature
 2. Food habits – Caribbean Area – Juvenile literature
 I. Title
 394.2'69729

ISBN 07502 2224 7

Typeset by Mark Whitchurch Art & Design
Printed and bound in Italy by EuroGrafica, Vicenza.

Find Wayland on the Internet at http://www.wayland.co.uk

CONTENTS

The Caribbean and its Food

United States

A T L A N T I C   O C E A N

The Caribbean

The Caribbean's place in the world

Nassau

BAHAMAS

Havana

CUBA

TURKS and
CAICOS ISLANDS

N

G R E A T E R   A N T I L L E S

DOMINICAN
REPUBLIC

LEEWARD ISLANDS

CAYMAN ISLANDS

HAITI

VIRGIN
ISLANDS

PUERTO
RICO

ANGUILLA
BARBUDA

Kingston

St CROIX

SABA

ANTIGUA

JAMAICA

HISPANIOLA

St KITTS and NEVIS
MONTSERRAT

GUADELOUPE

L E S S E R
A N T I L L E S

DOMINICA

MARTINIQUE

C A R I B B E A N   S E A

St LUCIA
BARBADOS

0   400 km

DUTCH
ANTILLES

WINDWARD ISLANDS

0   200 miles

ARUBA

St VINCENT and
the GRENADINES

GRENADA

TOBAGO
TRINIDAD

S O U T H   A M E R I C A

4

SUGAR CANE

Sugar cane was introduced to the Caribbean by European settlers. The juice of the sugar cane is used to make sugar, rum and a refreshing, sweet soft drink.

RICE

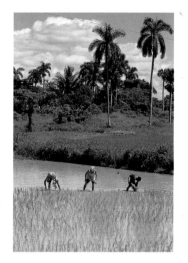

Rice is grown all over the Caribbean. It is one of many different foods which were brought to the Caribbean by Indian settlers.

FRUIT AND NUTS

The hot, Caribbean climate means that many different tropical fruits can be grown on the islands.

VEGETABLES

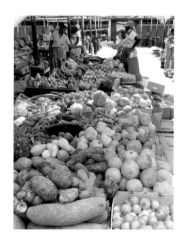

Root vegetables, such as yams and sweet potatoes, are an important part of the Caribbean diet. They were brought to the Caribbean from Africa.

FISH AND SEAFOOD

The Caribbean Sea is rich in fish and seafood, such as lobsters and crabs. Fish is cooked in many different ways.

SPICES

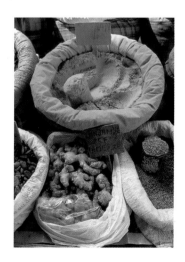

Ginger, nutmeg, peppers and allspice are grown in the Caribbean. They add flavour to many Caribbean dishes.

People, Food and Farming

▼ Once sugar cane has been harvested, it goes to factories to have the sweet juice crushed out of it.

The Caribbean is a region made up of over 30 large islands in the Caribbean Sea, between North and South America. It is in the tropics, so the climate is warm all year.

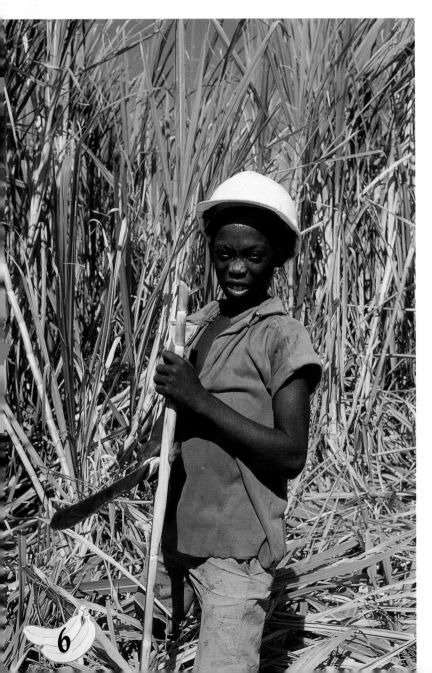

The people of the Caribbean are a mixture of many different cultures. The first people to live there were Arawak Indians. Then, 500 years ago, people from Spain, England, France and Holland settled in the Caribbean. They brought slaves from Western Africa to work on sugar and tobacco plantations. More recently, East Indians, Chinese and Arabs have settled there.

Each of these groups of people brought with them their traditional celebrations, their cooking and sometimes even the ingredients, which became part of the diet of Caribbean people.

Rice and bread

Rice and bread are very important in the Caribbean. Rice is used in dishes such as rice and peas, and with Indian curries and Chinese dishes.

Rice grows well in the tropical Caribbean climate because it needs rain and sunshine to grow. During most of the year the temperature stays between 25°C and 30°C and there is a rainy season between September and November.

There are lots of different types of bread in the Caribbean, but the most famous is the *dhalpourri*. This is a flat Indian bread made with ground split peas. It is filled with curried potatoes, meat, and chickpeas, and is rolled up and eaten like a sandwich.

Once rice has ▶ been picked, it is sieved to get rid of the husks, or shells, around each grain.

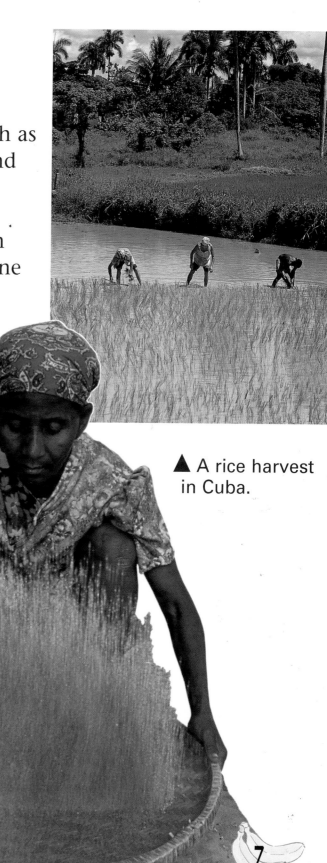

▲ A rice harvest in Cuba.

Tropical fruits

Caribbean people buy their fruit from large open markets. Some of the fruits, such as bananas, coconuts and mangoes, are sold abroad to countries like Britain.

Coconuts are very popular in the Caribbean. The 'milk' or juice inside is a refreshing drink and the kernel itself is used as an ingredient in many different dishes such as cakes, curries, sweets and sauces.

UNUSUAL FRUITS

You can see some Caribbean fruits, such as bananas and pineapples in your local shops. But others are more unusual. Breadfruit has bumpy, pale-green skin and a creamy flesh. Ackee has an orange skin with a bright yellow fruit. It is the main ingredient of the national dish of Jamaica, ackee and saltfish.

▼ The climate of the Caribbean means that tropical fruits like pineapples and watermelons grow all year round.

▲ Breadfruit trees can grow as tall as 18 metres high! Although breadfruit is a fruit, it is often cooked like a vegetable and used instead of potatoes or rice.

▼ Vegetables in the Caribbean come in all kinds of shapes, sizes and colours.

Vegetables

Lots of different vegetables grow in the Caribbean. Many of the islanders grow vegetables just for themselves, but much is sold abroad.

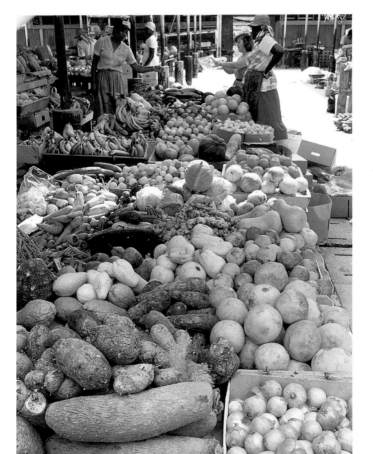

Vegetables are cooked in hundreds of different ways. Caribbean cooks often mix both sweet and savoury ingredients in their food. Sweet potatoes are sometimes cooked in sugar (see recipe on page 19), or mashed. Yams are cooked like potatoes. Cassava can be made into a kind of flour, or eaten as a vegetable. Callaloo is like spinach and is used in a dish called pepperpot soup.

▲ Barbecued fish.

▼ Fishing is an important industry in the Caribbean.

Seafood

People in the Caribbean can choose from fish such as clams, lobster, tuna, snapper, shark, conch and mullet. Fish and seafood is used in festival foods, as well as everyday dishes. It is barbecued, curried or cooked in the traditional Caribbean style of 'jerk'. Jerk fish, beef or chicken is made by flavouring the fish or meat with a peppery sauce and then barbecuing it.

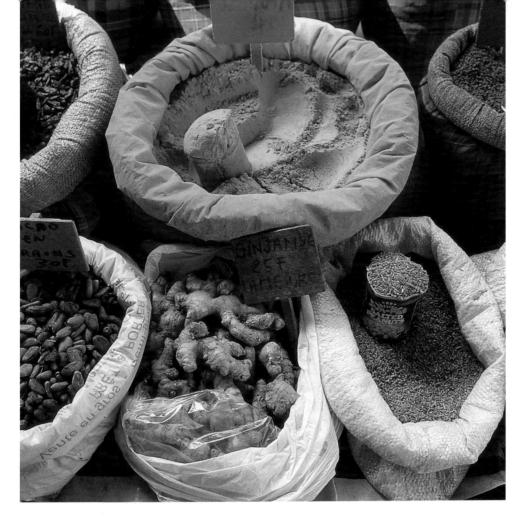

◄ Brightly coloured spices are bought by weight from open-air markets and shops throughout the Caribbean.

Spices

Wherever you go in the Caribbean, spices are usually used to flavour food. The mixture of spices varies from island to island. In Trinidad, people use *massala* in their dishes. This is a mixture of coriander seeds, anise, cloves, cumin, fenugreek, peppercorns, mustard and turmeric. Peppers are one of the most famous spices used in Caribbean cookery. Pepper sauces are made from hot, yellow peppers that grow all over the islands, and each cook has a different way of preparing the sauce.

HISTORY THROUGH FOOD

Caribbean dishes can tell you about the history of the islands. For example, *foo-foo*, *coo-coo* and *dunckunoo* (dishes made from plantain and okra) came from West Africa. Escovitched fish (marinated fish) is found in islands that were Spanish colonies, and *fricassee de poulet au coco* (chicken in coconut milk) is cooked on islands that were French.

Caribbean Religions

There are many different religions in the Caribbean. Most people are Christians – mainly Roman Catholics or Anglicans. There are also many people that follow versions of African religions, such as Voodoo, Pocomania and Santeria. In the Caribbean, however, these religions have been mixed with Christianity. In some countries, like Guyana and Trinidad, the Hindu and Muslim religions are also very popular.

▲ During the Santeria festival of Shango, beautifully prepared food is laid out on an altar as a religious offering.

◄ For Christians at this church in Barbados, the visit to church is a social as well as religious time.

Festivals and food

The food and festivals of the Caribbean reflect the many different religions and cultures there. A festival might be a celebration of a Muslim tradition, such as Id-ul-Fitr, which marks the end of Ramadan. But the food that is served can be any style, from Chinese to Brazilian! The one thing that all Caribbean cooking uses is fresh ingredients.

RASTAFARIANISM

In Jamaica there is a religion called Rastafarianism, which does not allow its followers to eat pork meat or fish without scales. Many Rastafarians are vegetarian or vegan. *Ital* food is a vegetarian type of cooking introduced by Rastafarians. It includes things like vegetable patties and it is now becoming popular in the Caribbean.

▲ This Rastafarian family in Jamaica wear the red, green and gold colours of their religion. The man is also wearing the dreadlock hairstyle that many Rastafarians wear.

13

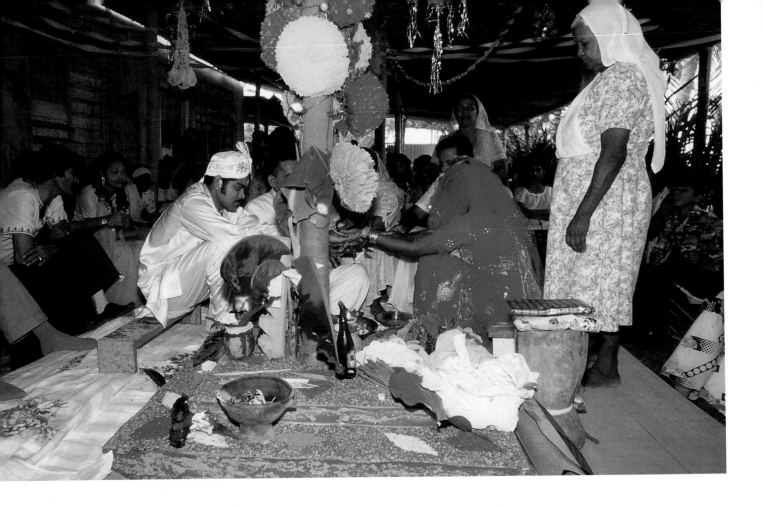

▲ At this Hindu wedding in Trinidad, the bride is wearing a traditional red *sari*. Offerings of food, such as rice, are made to Hindu gods throughout the ceremony.

Food and celebrations

Food is an important part of most religious celebrations in the Caribbean. Voodoo followers, when asking for a favour from a spirit or 'Iwa', make offerings of cake and grilled corn. In a traditional Hindu wedding, only vegetarian food is served, but in Christian weddings it is common to eat meat dishes, such as curried lamb. There is a recipe for curried lamb on the opposite page.

◀ Curried lamb, with a selection of spices.

Curried Lamb

EQUIPMENT

Large saucepan   Wooden spoon

Knife   Chopping board

INGREDIENTS

30 g Olive oil

500 g Lamb, cut into cubes

2 Large onions, finely sliced

2 Teaspoons curry powder

1 Tablespoon freshly grated coconut or desiccated coconut

$1/2$ Teaspoon allspice

1 Lamb stock cube mixed in 600 ml of water

1 Bay leaf

Pinch of cayenne pepper

Salt and a dash of Tabasco sauce

Ask an adult to heat the oil in the saucepan. Add the meat and fry for about 5 minutes. Take it out and put into a bowl.

In the same pan, fry the onions until soft. Stir in the curry powder, allspice and coconut and cook for a few minutes.

Add the lamb stock, bay leaf, cayenne pepper and the fried meat. Cover and simmer for 2 hours.

Taste and add more salt if needed. If using Tabasco sauce, stir in just before serving.

Be careful when frying. Ask an adult to help you.

Christmas and New Year

Christmas and New Year are celebrated all over the Caribbean. This is the season of bamboo bursting, when bamboo poles are filled with gunpowder and snapped, to sound like firecrackers. Lots of special dishes are prepared.

▼ Many of the traditions of Christmas that we know in Britain, such as Santa Claus, are also popular in the Caribbean.

Ham, turkey or a whole roasted pig or goat are some of the traditional Christmas foods served on many of the islands. Caribbean people also eat a Christmas cake very similar to the British one, but flavoured with rum.

SCOTTISH FOOD

Another European Christmas recipe is *jug jug*, which is a kind of pastie made from pork and beef. It is said to have come from Scotland originally.

Professional dancers in the ▶ Caribbean putting on a traditional dance for tourists. Dancing is an important part of Christmas celebrations.

Jonkonnu and Papa Jab

Christmas and New Year are also marked by parades. Pipes, cowbells, whistles, foghorns and drums, announce the arrival of the Jonkonnu (or John Canoe) dancers. The dancers are dressed in different costumes as animals, kings and funny characters, and their dancing pattern tells stories that have been passed down from one generation to the next.

Papa Jab is a folk character from St Lucia. During the New Year celebrations, someone dresses up as Papa Jab and joins groups of people in masks and costumes, singing and dancing through the streets. Children are scared of Papa Jab because legend has it that he will eat badly behaved children!

▲ Candied sweet potatoes is a favourite savoury dish in the Caribbean. There is a recipe for this dish on the opposite page.

HAPPY NEW YEAR

In Jamaica, there is a belief that to make sure you have a good year, the first thing that you eat in the New Year should be roasted suckling pig.

Candied Sweet Potatoes

EQUIPMENT

2 Saucepans
Chopping board
Wooden spoon
Knife

Baking dish, greased
Colander
Oven gloves

1 Turn the oven on to a medium temperature. Ask an adult to boil the potatoes for about 10 minutes. Drain and leave to cool. Cut into thick slices.

2 Put the orange peel in the second saucepan with the butter, sugar and water. Cook over a low flame, stirring constantly for 5 minutes, or until the sugar has melted and the mixture has thickened.

3 Arrange the sweet potatoes in the baking dish. Pour the orange syrup over them, making sure they are all coated evenly.

4 Put the dish in the oven and bake for 30 minutes or until browned. Ask an adult to take the potatoes out of the oven.

Always use oven gloves to take hot dishes from ovens. Ask an adult to help you.

Carnival

Carnival began as a Christian festival. It originally took place just before Lent, when Christians had to fast and avoid certain foods, such as meat. This is how the festival got its name – the word 'carnival' comes from the Latin words *'carne levare'*, which means 'to take away meat'.

▼ The steel drums are probably the most famous sound in the Caribbean. They were invented in Trinidad.

French settlers introduced Carnival to the Caribbean several hundred years ago. Later, it was celebrated by African slaves. The slaves tried to forget how hard their lives were at carnival time. They made fun of their masters by dressing up and copying them.

Carnival is still a time for dancing, playing music and dressing up in the Caribbean. Each costume is carefully designed, and a King and Queen of the Carnival are chosen from hundreds of masked people.

Costumes are decorated with satin, beads, feathers, plastic and they are made using wonderfully patterned materials. Some costumes are traditional to particular islands, such as the She Devils of Martinique, or the six-metre-high Mocko Jumbies of Saint Thomas.

▼ Preparations for the Carnival take months. Clothes and models have to be made and tried out so that everything is perfect for the big event.

Party time

▲ The parades at Carnival are usually really long, and it takes the Carnival-goers hours to make their way through the streets.

▼ Fried chicken is sold all over the Caribbean, and each family has a different mixture of spices to season the flour. Some like it spicy, others like it plain.

Carnival is celebrated on most of the islands, and at different times of the year. In Curacao it takes place in January, while in Antigua it is in late July. The most famous carnival is in Trinidad and Tobago. It starts at 4 am on the Monday before Ash Wednesday and continues for 48 hours! During this time thousands of people march and dance in the streets to the rhythm of steel bands. There are stalls selling delicious food, such as fried chicken, *rotis* filled with chicken or stewed beef, and vegetable fritters.

Sweet treats

Many of the foods sold at Carnival time are very sugary. Sweets and cakes made with coconut and honey are sold on roadside stalls.

▲ Sorrel drink is a refreshing Carnival drink. It is made from dried sorrel flowers mixed with water, ginger, orange and sugar.

Tamarind balls are made from sugar, salt and tamarind fruit and they have a tangy flavour. *Bulla* is made using ginger grown on the islands. It is a sweet cake that is a real favourite of children, especially in Jamaica.

Drinks are sweet, too. There is a green drink made from sugar cane, which is very refreshing. Chilled coconut milk is also popular.

◀ Coconut milk is best drunk straight from the shell.

Children's Carnival

In Trinidad and Tobago there is a children's carnival, which is just as colourful and exciting as the main carnival. Children dance and take part in competitions to see who is wearing the best costume.

▲ Children love taking part in the Carnival because it's a good opportunity for singing, dancing and having fun.

Fried Chicken

EQUIPMENT
Sieve
Bowl
Plate
Frying pan
Whisk

INGREDIENTS

4 Pieces of chicken   Salt and pepper
2 Eggs   Oil
100 g flour

Crack the eggs into a bowl and beat them well.

Add a pinch of salt and pepper to the flour and then sieve the mixture on to the plate.

Dip each of the chicken pieces into the beaten egg. Then roll them in the flour. Ask an adult to heat up enough oil in a frying pan to cover the chicken completely.

Once the oil is hot, add the chicken pieces one by one. Cook until they are brown on the outside and white on the inside.

Ask an adult to do the frying. Hot oil can be very dangerous.

Food and Harvest Festivals

Some festivals in the Caribbean celebrate the harvest of crops, or other food.

In St Lucia, there is a fishing festival held every year on Saint Peter's Day, which is on 29 June. Fishermen give thanks to Saint Peter and Saint Paul. Their brightly painted fishing boats and boat sheds are blessed, and there is a special mass. Saltfish cakes are a favourite dish.

▲ Saltfish cakes are a favourite dish at festival time. There is a recipe for them on page 29.

◄ Colourful fishing boats in the fishing village of Anse le Raye, in St Lucia.

Crop Over

Many islands have a festival called Crop Over. This is a type of harvest festival which was started by slaves to celebrate the end of the sugar-cane harvest.

Barbados has the most famous Crop Over. There are fairs, concerts, cart parades and other activities, including a Calypso competition and the crowning of the Calypso King.

▼ Crop Over festival in Barbados is celebrated with special stilt dancing.

Phagwa

Phagwa (pronounced 'pag-wa') is a Hindu festival which is celebrated in Trinidad, Guyana and Surinam. It was brought to the Caribbean by Indian settlers, and is similar to the Indian festival of Holi.

Phagwa, like Holi, is a spring festival, which is held near the full moon in March. It celebrates the arrival of spring and the new growth of crops and flowers.

In Trinidad, people go to parks and throw or spray coloured powder over each other. They dance and sing folk and other religious songs.

▼ These girls are celebrating Phagwa in Trinidad.

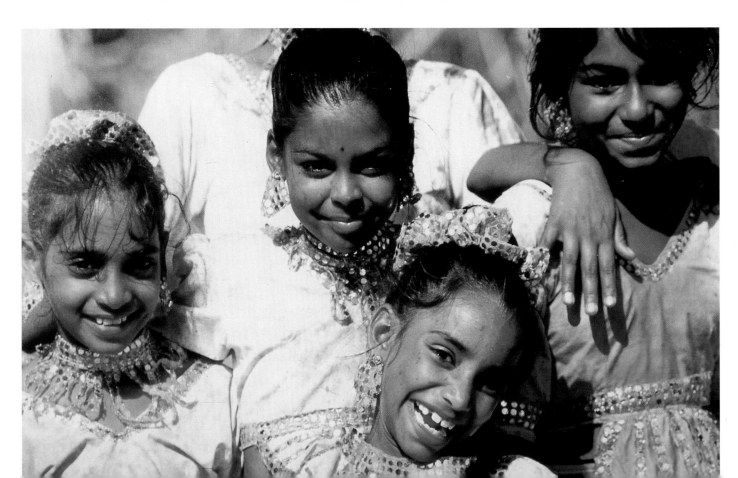

Saltfish Cakes

EQUIPMENT

Food processor
Large saucepan
Plate
Frying pan

INGREDIENTS

200 g Salted fish (cod)
3 Potatoes, peeled and boiled
1 Onion, chopped
1 Clove garlic, chopped
1 Egg

2 Tablespoons spring onions, chopped
1 Teaspoon fresh parsley, chopped
Pepper to taste
3 Tablespoons flour
Oil

① Wash the fish and soak it in cold water overnight. Cover with fresh water and boil for 10 minutes. Once it has cooled, remove the skin and bones.

② Put the potatoes, onion, garlic, spring onions, parsley, egg and pepper into a food processor and mix well.

③ Take a handful of the mixture at a time and press it into small cakes. Once you have used all the mixture, coat each fish cake with flour.

④ Ask an adult to heat the oil in a frying pan and fry the fish cakes for about 8 minutes, until they are golden brown.

Always be careful with frying. Ask an adult to help you.

Glossary

Anglican   One of the beliefs within the Church of England.

Ash Wednesday   The first day of Lent.

Calypso   A type of song that comes from the West Indies.

Christians   People who believe in Jesus Christ.

Colonisers   People who settle together in other countries.

Cuttings   Pieces cut from a plant.

Fasting   To give up eating and drinking.

Fertile   Land that is good for growing crops.

Hinduism   A major Indian religion, which is based on the belief that God has many forms.

Hurricanes   Very strong storms, which cause a lot of damage.

Id-ul-fitr   A Muslim ceremony which marks the end of Ramadan.

Mocko Jumbies   Dancers from Saint Thomas, who stand on stilts that make them 6 metres high.

Muslim   Somebody who follows the Islamic religion, who believes in one God, Allah.

Rastafarianism   A religion from Jamaica, which involves the worship of the old emperor of Ethiopia, Ras Tafari, as God.

Roman Catholicism   The Christian Church that is led by the Pope.

Rotis   Flat, Indian bread.

Sari   A piece of clothing from India. It is a long piece of cloth that is wrapped around the body like a dress and worn by women.

Vegan   Somebody who does not eat meat, fish or any animal products such as dairy products.

Vegetarian   Somebody who does not eat meat or fish.

Photograph and artwork acknowledgements
Andes Press Agency 5 (top right), p7 (top); Axiom Photographic Agency 5 (middle left), 5 (middle right), 8, 9 (botom); Eye Ubiquitous 5 (bottom right), 11, 13, 27 (Mike Alkins); Robert Harding 9 (top); John and Penny Hubley 14 (top); Hutchinson Library 3, 23 (bottom) Eric Ayrs; Impact 7 (bottom), 24 (bottom); James Davis 1, 10 (bottom), 17; Norton Studios, Trinidad 28; Panos 5 (left top), 6, 12 (top); Betty Press 20; South American Pictures 21; St Lucia Tourist Board 16, 26 (bottom); Trip 22 (T. Bogna), 12 (A. Tovey); Zul Mukhida 14, 18, 26 (top).

Topic Web and Resources

MATHS Using and understanding data and measures (recipes). Using and understanding fractions. Using and reading measuring instruments: scales.	**SCIENCE** Food and nutrition. Plants in different habitats. Separating mixtures of materials: sieving and dissolving. Changing materials through heat.	**GEOGRAPHY** Locality study. Weather. Farming. Comparing physical landscapes. Influence of landscape on human activities: farming and food festivals. How land is used.

DESIGN AND TECHNOLOGY
Design and make a cereal box.
Design a poster to advertise a food product.
Technology used in food production.
Packaging.

Food & Festivals
TOPIC WEB

HISTORY
Trace the history of modern British food.
Investigate the different farming methods used over the past century.

ENGLISH
Make up a slogan to sell a food product.
Write a poem or story using food as the subject.
Write a list of food words and non-food words.
Write a menu you might find in a Caribbean restaurant.

MODERN FOREIGN LANGUAGES
Language skills.
Everyday activities: food.
People, places and customs.

BOOKS TO READ

Caribbean Carnival, Songs of the West Indies by Irving Bugie (Macmillan 1993)

Traditions from the Caribbean by Paul Dash (Wayland 1998)

Caribbean Stories by Robert Hull (Wayland 1994)

A Taste of the Caribbean by Yvonne McKenley (Wayland 1994)

GAMES

Multicultural Food Fun (NES Arnold, Nottingham): Young children can match food to their country of origin.

This book meets the following specific objectives of the National Literacy Strategy's Framework for Teaching:

☑ Range of non-fiction text: simple recipes (Year 2 Term 1 & Year 3 Term 2), instructions, labels, captions, lists, glossary, index.

☑ Vocabulary extension: words linked to particular topics (food words) and technical words from work in other subjects (geography and food science).

Index

Page numbers in **bold** mean there is a photograph on the page.